PRAYER AND GRATITUDE JOURNAL

An Inspirational Guide with Journal Prompts and Motivational Quotes

PRAYER AND GRATITUDE JOURNAL

An Inspirational Guide with Journal Prompts and Motivational Quotes

@2021 Andrea Clarke Pratt

All rights reserved. No portion of this book may be reproduced in any form without permission from the publisher, except as permitted by U.S. copyright law. For permissions contact: adpratt6@gmail.com

Unless otherwise indicated, scripture quotations taken from the King James Version (KJV) - public domain.

Printed in the United States of America

ISBN-978-1-63877-379-5

CONGRATULATIONS! You have made a decision to express your gratitude and thanksgiving to God through journaling and this will indeed have a positive impact upon your life.

This Daily Prayer and Gratitude Journal is a wonderful way to commune with God and give Him gratitude for the blessings He bestows and to worship him for who He is.

In this journal you will find:

*Scripture Verses
*Insightful Journal Prompts
*Inspirational Quotes
*Space for Reflections
*Gratitude Prompt
Beautiful color format

Also included in this Prayer and Gratitude Journal are prompts for prayers of Adoration, Confession, Thanksgiving and Supplication (ACTS)

LET US BEGIN!

SCRIPTURE OF THE WEEK

"Bless the Lord, O my soul, and forget not all his benefits,
Who forgiveth all thine iniquities;
Who healeth all thy diseases,
Who redeemeth thy life from destruction;
Who crowneth thee with lovingkindness and tender mercies,
who satisfieth thy mouth with good things;
so that thy youth is renewed like the eagle's".

Psalm 103:2-5

QUOTE OF THE WEEK

Thankfulness is the beginning of gratitude. Gratitude is the completion of thankfulness. Thankfulness may consist merely of words. Gratitude is shown in acts...
Henri Frederic Amiel

THE GRATEFUL LEPER

"And one of them, when he saw that he was healed, turned back, and with a loud voice glorified God, And fell down on his face at his feet, giving him thanks: and he was a Samaritan."
Luke 17:15-16

My Bible Verse for Today

Date:..........................

_____
_____
_____

My Reflections for Today

_____
_____
_____
_____
_____
_____
_____
_____
_____

Lord, today I am grateful for the following persons and divine helpers you have placed in my life

_____
_____
_____
_____

Lord, today I am grateful for the following things you have given to me

_____
_____
_____
_____

Lord, you deserve my worship and adoration because

_____
_____
_____
_____

My Bible Verse for Today

Date:..............................

_____
_____
_____

My Reflections for Today

_____
_____
_____
_____
_____
_____
_____
_____
_____

Lord, today I am grateful for the following persons and divine helpers you have placed in my life

_____

_____

_____

_____

Lord, today I am grateful for the following things you have given to me

_____

_____

_____

_____

Lord, you deserve my worship and adoration because

_____

_____

_____

_____

My Bible Verse for Today

Date:....................................

_____
_____
_____

My Reflections for Today

_____
_____
_____
_____
_____
_____
_____
_____

Lord, today I am grateful for the following persons and divine helpers you have placed in my life

_____
_____
_____
_____

Lord, today I am grateful for the following things you have given to me

_____
_____
_____
_____

Lord, you deserve my worship and adoration because

_____
_____
_____
_____

My Bible Verse for Today

Date:........................

_____
_____
_____

My Reflections for Today

_____
_____
_____
_____
_____
_____
_____
_____
_____

Lord, today I am grateful for the following persons and divine helpers you have placed in my life

_____
_____
_____
_____

Lord, today I am grateful for the following things you have given to me

_____
_____
_____
_____

Lord, you deserve my worship and adoration because

_____
_____
_____
_____

My Bible Verse for Today

Date:..............................

_____
_____
_____

My Reflections for Today

_____
_____
_____
_____
_____
_____
_____
_____
_____

Lord, today I am grateful for the following persons and divine helpers you have placed in my life

_____
_____
_____
_____

Lord, today I am grateful for the following things you have given to me

_____
_____
_____
_____

Lord, you deserve my worship and adoration because

_____
_____
_____
_____

My Bible Verse for Today

Date:..............................

_____

_____

_____

My Reflections for Today

_____

_____

_____

_____

_____

_____

_____

_____

Lord, today I am grateful for the following persons and divine helpers you have placed in my life

_____
_____
_____
_____

Lord, today I am grateful for the following things you have given to me

_____
_____
_____
_____

Lord, you deserve my worship and adoration because

_____
_____
_____
_____

My Bible Verse for Today

Date:.............................

_____
_____
_____

My Reflections for Today

_____
_____
_____
_____
_____
_____
_____

Lord, today I am grateful for the following persons and divine helpers you have placed in my life

_____

_____

_____

_____

Lord, today I am grateful for the following things you have given to me

_____

_____

_____

_____

Lord, you deserve my worship and adoration because

_____

_____

_____

_____

ACTS

Adoration

Give God praise and honor for who He is

"Thou art worthy, O Lord, to receive glory and honour and power: for thou hast created all things, and for thy pleasure they are and were created." Revelations 4:11

_____

_____

_____

Confession

Confess your sins to God

"If we confess our sins, He is Faithful and Just to forgive us our sins and to cleanse us from all unrighteousness. 1 John 1:9

_____

_____

_____

ACTS

Thanksgiving

Thank God for all of the blessings He has given to you.

O give thanks unto the Lord; for he is good: for his mercy endureth for ever. Psalms 136:1

_____

_____

_____

_____

Supplication

Pray for your needs and the needs of others

Be careful for nothing; but in every thing by prayer and supplication with thanksgiving let your requests be made known unto God. Philippians 4:6

_____

_____

_____

_____

SCRIPTURE OF THE WEEK

"In every thing give thanks: for this is the will of God in Christ Jesus concerning you."

1 Thessalonians 5:18

QUOTE OF THE WEEK

Train your mind and heart to see the good in everything. There is always something to be thankful for.

JOB WAS THANKFUL DESPITE LOSING SO MUCH

"And said, Naked came I out of my mother's womb, and naked shall I return thither: the LORD gave, and the LORD hath taken away; blessed be the name of the LORD."
JOB 1:21

Date:_ _ _ _ _ _ _ _ _ _

My Bible Verse for Today

_____

_____

_____

_____

My Reflections for Today

_____

_____

_____

_____

_____

_____

_____

_____

Lord, today I am grateful for the following persons and divine helpers you have placed in my life

_____
_____
_____
_____

Lord, today I am grateful for the following things you have given to me

_____
_____
_____
_____

Lord, you deserve my worship and adoration because

_____
_____
_____
_____

Date:_ _ _ _ _ _ _ _ _ _

My Bible Verse for Today

_____

_____

_____

_____

My Reflections for Today

_____

_____

_____

_____

_____

_____

_____

_____

_____

Lord, today I am grateful for the following persons and divine helpers you have placed in my life

_____
_____
_____
_____

Lord, today I am grateful for the following things you have given to me

_____
_____
_____
_____

Lord, you deserve my worship and adoration because

_____
_____
_____
_____

Date:_ _ _ _ _ _ _ _ _ _

My Bible Verse for Today

_____
_____
_____
_____

My Reflections for Today

_____
_____
_____
_____
_____
_____
_____
_____
_____

Lord, today I am grateful for the following persons and divine helpers you have placed in my life

_____
_____
_____
_____

Lord, today I am grateful for the following things you have given to me

_____
_____
_____
_____

Lord, you deserve my worship and adoration because

_____
_____
_____
_____

Date:_ _ _ _ _ _ _ _ _ _

My Bible Verse for Today

_____
_____
_____
_____
_____

My Reflections for Today

_____
_____
_____
_____
_____
_____
_____
_____
_____

Lord, today I am grateful for the following persons and divine helpers you have placed in my life

_____

_____

_____

_____

Lord, today I am grateful for the following things you have given to me

_____

_____

_____

_____

Lord, you deserve my worship and adoration because

_____

_____

_____

_____

Date:_ _ _ _ _ _ _ _ _ _

My Bible Verse for Today

_____
_____
_____
_____
_____

My Reflections for Today

_____
_____
_____
_____
_____
_____
_____
_____
_____

Lord, today I am grateful for the following persons and divine helpers you have placed in my life

_____

_____

_____

_____

Lord, today I am grateful for the following things you have given to me

_____

_____

_____

_____

Lord, you deserve my worship and adoration because

_____

_____

_____

_____

Date:_____

My Bible Verse for Today

_____
_____
_____
_____

My Reflections for Today

_____
_____
_____
_____
_____
_____
_____
_____

Lord, today I am grateful for the following persons and divine helpers you have placed in my life

_____

_____

_____

_____

Lord, today I am grateful for the following things you have given to me

_____

_____

_____

_____

Lord, you deserve my worship and adoration because

_____

_____

_____

_____

Date:_ _ _ _ _ _ _ _ _ _

My Bible Verse for Today

_____
_____
_____
_____

My Reflections for Today

_____
_____
_____
_____
_____
_____
_____
_____

Lord, today I am grateful for the following persons and divine helpers you have placed in my life

_____
_____
_____
_____

Lord, today I am grateful for the following things you have given to me

_____
_____
_____
_____

Lord, you deserve my worship and adoration because

_____
_____
_____
_____

ACTS

Adoration

Give God praise and honor for who He is

"Thou art worthy, O Lord, to receive glory and honour and power: for thou hast created all things, and for thy pleasure they are and were created." Revelations 4:11

_____

_____

_____

Confession

Confess your sins to God

"If we confess our sins, He is Faithful and Just to forgive us our sins and to cleanse us from all unrighteousness. 1 John 1:9

_____

_____

_____

ACTS

Thanksgiving

Thank God for all of the blessings He has given to you.

O give thanks unto the Lord; for he is good: for his mercy endureth for ever. Psalms 136:1

_____

_____

_____

_____

Supplication

Pray for your needs and the needs of others

Be careful for nothing; but in every thing by prayer and supplication with thanksgiving let your requests be made known unto God. Philippians 4:6

_____

_____

_____

_____

QUOTE OF THE WEEK

All the great things are simple, and many can be expressed in a single word: freedom, justice, honor, duty, mercy, hope...
Winston Churchill

MOSES AND THE CHILDREN OF ISRAEL PRAISE GOD FOR DELIVERANCE FROM THE ENEMY

Thy right hand, O LORD, is become glorious in power: thy right hand, O LORD, hath dashed in pieces the enemy.

Exodus 15:6

Date:_ _ _ _ _ _ _ _ _ _

My Bible Verse for Today

_____
_____
_____
_____

My Reflections for Today

_____
_____
_____
_____
_____
_____
_____
_____

Lord, today I am grateful for the following persons and divine helpers you have placed in my life

_____

_____

_____

_____

Lord, today I am grateful for the following things you have given to me

_____

_____

_____

_____

Lord, you deserve my worship and adoration because

_____

_____

_____

_____

Date:_ _ _ _ _ _ _ _ _ _

My Bible Verse for Today

_____
_____
_____
_____
_____

My Reflections for Today

_____
_____
_____
_____
_____
_____
_____
_____
_____

Lord, today I am grateful for the following persons and divine helpers you have placed in my life

_____

_____

_____

Lord, today I am grateful for the following things you have given to me

_____

_____

_____

Lord, you deserve my worship and adoration because

_____

_____

_____

Date:_____

My Bible Verse for Today

_____
_____
_____
_____
_____

My Reflections for Today

_____
_____
_____
_____
_____
_____
_____
_____
_____
_____

Lord, today I am grateful for the following persons and divine helpers you have placed in my life

_____

_____

_____

_____

Lord, today I am grateful for the following things you have given to me

_____

_____

_____

_____

Lord, you deserve my worship and adoration because

_____

_____

_____

_____

Date:_____

My Bible Verse for Today

_____
_____
_____
_____

My Reflections for Today

_____
_____
_____
_____
_____
_____
_____
_____

Lord, today I am grateful for the following persons and divine helpers you have placed in my life

_____

_____

_____

_____

Lord, today I am grateful for the following things you have given to me

_____

_____

_____

_____

Lord, you deserve my worship and adoration because

_____

_____

_____

_____

Date:_____

My Bible Verse for Today

_____
_____
_____
_____

My Reflections for Today

_____
_____
_____
_____
_____
_____
_____
_____

Lord, today I am grateful for the following persons and divine helpers you have placed in my life

_____
_____
_____
_____

Lord, today I am grateful for the following things you have given to me

_____
_____
_____
_____

Lord, you deserve my worship and adoration because

_____
_____
_____
_____

Date:_ _ _ _ _ _ _ _ _ _

My Bible Verse for Today

_____
_____
_____
_____
_____

My Reflections for Today

_____
_____
_____
_____
_____
_____
_____
_____
_____
_____

Lord, today I am grateful for the following persons and divine helpers you have placed in my life

_____

_____

_____

_____

Lord, today I am grateful for the following things you have given to me

_____

_____

_____

_____

Lord, you deserve my worship and adoration because

_____

_____

_____

_____

Date:_ _ _ _ _ _ _ _ _ _

My Bible Verse for Today

_____
_____
_____
_____

My Reflections for Today

_____
_____
_____
_____
_____
_____
_____
_____
_____

Lord, today I am grateful for the following persons and divine helpers you have placed in my life

_____

_____

_____

Lord, today I am grateful for the following things you have given to me

_____

_____

_____

Lord, you deserve my worship and adoration because

_____

_____

_____

ACTS

Adoration

Give God praise and honor for who He is

"Thou art worthy, O Lord, to receive glory and honour and power: for thou hast created all things, and for thy pleasure they are and were created." Revelations 4:11

_____

_____

_____

Confession

Confess your sins to God

"If we confess our sins, He is Faithful and Just to forgive us our sins and to cleanse us from all unrighteousness. 1 John 1:9

_____

_____

_____

ACTS

Thanksgiving

Thank God for all of the blessings He has given to you.

O give thanks unto the Lord; for he is good: for his mercy endureth for ever. Psalms 136:1

_____

_____

_____

_____

Supplication

Pray for your needs and the needs of others

Be careful for nothing; but in every thing by prayer and supplication with thanksgiving let your requests be made known unto God. Philippians 4:6

_____

_____

_____

_____

SCRIPTURE OF THE WEEK

But he was wounded for our transgressions, he was bruised for our iniquities: the chastisement of our peace was upon him; and with his stripes we are healed.

All we like sheep have gone astray; we have turned every one to his own way; and the Lord hath laid on him the iniquity of us all.

He was oppressed, and he was afflicted, yet he opened not his mouth: he is brought as a lamb to the slaughter, and as a sheep before her shearers is dumb, so he openeth not his mouth.

Isaiah 53:5-8

QUOTE OF THE WEEK

How grateful we should be that Christ our Lord and King has redeemed us from the curse of sin.
Andrea Clarke Pratt

JOB IS GRATEFUL FOR THE REDEEMER

"For I know that my redeemer liveth, and that he shall stand at the latter day upon the earth"

Job 19:25

Date:_____

My Bible Verse for Today

_____
_____
_____
_____

My Reflections for Today

_____
_____
_____
_____
_____
_____
_____
_____

Lord, today I am grateful for the following persons and divine helpers you have placed in my life

_____
_____
_____
_____

Lord, today I am grateful for the following things you have given to me

_____
_____
_____
_____

Lord, you deserve my worship and adoration because

_____
_____
_____
_____

Date:_ _ _ _ _ _ _ _ _ _

My Bible Verse for Today

_____
_____
_____
_____
_____

My Reflections for Today

_____
_____
_____
_____
_____
_____
_____
_____
_____
_____

Lord, today I am grateful for the following persons and divine helpers you have placed in my life

_____

_____

_____

_____

Lord, today I am grateful for the following things you have given to me

_____

_____

_____

_____

Lord, you deserve my worship and adoration because

_____

_____

_____

_____

Date:_ _ _ _ _ _ _ _ _ _

My Bible Verse for Today

_____

_____

_____

_____

_____

My Reflections for Today

_____

_____

_____

_____

_____

_____

_____

_____

_____

_____

Lord, today I am grateful for the following persons and divine helpers you have placed in my life

_____
_____
_____
_____

Lord, today I am grateful for the following things you have given to me

_____
_____
_____
_____

Lord, you deserve my worship and adoration because

_____
_____
_____
_____

Date:_ _ _ _ _ _ _ _ _ _

My Bible Verse for Today

_____
_____
_____
_____
_____

My Reflections for Today

_____
_____
_____
_____
_____
_____
_____
_____

Lord, today I am grateful for the following persons and divine helpers you have placed in my life

_____
_____
_____
_____

Lord, today I am grateful for the following things you have given to me

_____
_____
_____
_____

Lord, you deserve my worship and adoration because

_____
_____
_____
_____

Date:_____

My Bible Verse for Today

_____
_____
_____
_____
_____

My Reflections for Today

_____
_____
_____
_____
_____
_____
_____
_____
_____
_____

Lord, today I am grateful for the following persons and divine helpers you have placed in my life

_____
_____
_____
_____

Lord, today I am grateful for the following things you have given to me

_____
_____
_____
_____

Lord, you deserve my worship and adoration because

_____
_____
_____
_____

Date:_ _ _ _ _ _ _ _ _ _

My Bible Verse for Today

_____
_____
_____
_____

My Reflections for Today

_____
_____
_____
_____
_____
_____
_____
_____

Lord, today I am grateful for the following persons and divine helpers you have placed in my life

_____
_____
_____
_____

Lord, today I am grateful for the following things you have given to me

_____
_____
_____
_____

Lord, you deserve my worship and adoration because

_____
_____
_____
_____

Date:_ _ _ _ _ _ _ _ _ _

My Bible Verse for Today

_____
_____
_____
_____
_____

My Reflections for Today

_____
_____
_____
_____
_____
_____
_____
_____
_____

Lord, today I am grateful for the following persons and divine helpers you have placed in my life

_____
_____
_____
_____

Lord, today I am grateful for the following things you have given to me

_____
_____
_____
_____

Lord, you deserve my worship and adoration because

_____
_____
_____
_____

ACTS

Adoration

Give God praise and honor for who He is

"Thou art worthy, O Lord, to receive glory and honour and power: for thou hast created all things, and for thy pleasure they are and were created." Revelations 4:11

_____

_____

_____

Confession

Confess your sins to God

"If we confess our sins, He is Faithful and Just to forgive us our sins and to cleanse us from all unrighteousness. 1 John 1:9

_____

_____

_____

ACTS

Thanksgiving

Thank God for all of the blessings He has given to you.

O give thanks unto the Lord; for he is good: for his mercy endureth for ever. Psalms 136:1

_____

_____

_____

_____

Supplication

Pray for your needs and the needs of others

Be careful for nothing; but in every thing by prayer and supplication with thanksgiving let your requests be made known unto God. Philippians 4:6

_____

_____

_____

_____

NOTES

_____

_____

_____

_____

_____

_____

_____

_____

_____

_____

NOTES

NOTES

_____

_____

_____

_____

_____

_____

_____

_____

_____

About the Author

Andrea Clarke Pratt retired in 2018 after more than 20 years in the corporate world. She then pursued the field of Education and is currently teaching at a High School. Her hunger for the Word of God led her to complete a Master's Degree in Theology.

Andrea is the Author of other prayer journals, educational books for children, and the book "I'm Loving My Age: A Believer's Guide to Aging Gracefully and Words of Hope for the Elderly."

www.ingramcontent.com/pod-product-compliance
Lightning Source LLC
LaVergne TN
LVHW021944060526
838200LV00042B/1920